MW00877643

Screenwriting for Anyone

How you can write your own screenplay in 30 days

(4 in 1 Book Box Set)

By George Lucas

Table of Contents

Book I
Write a Screenplay in 30 Days

6 Easy Steps to Get Started

By George Lucas

Introduction

I want to thank you and congratulate you for downloading the book, *"Write a Screenplay in 30 days – 6 Easy Steps to Get Started."*

This book contains proven steps and strategies on how to get started on the path to completing a full feature length screenplay in 30 days.

Have you always had an idea you know will make a great movie but you've never had the time or skills to write it out? This book will teach you the necessary steps to getting started on your screenplay in a fast and easy way. It will show you how to create a strong concept, unique characters, and a solid outline that will launch your idea and prepare you for taking the plunge into writing your feature length script. This book is the first is a series that is designed to guide you on your creative journey and helpful hints on how to speed up the process.

Thanks again for purchasing this book, I hope you enjoy it!

Chapter 1:
Write what you know

Mark Twain said it best in his novel The Adventures of Huckleberry Finn: write what you know. When it comes to screenwriting, it's as simple as that. We all have a unique story to tell and drawing inspiration from your life adds a personal quality that can't be replicated into your work. If you are an expert in something, then let that knowledge seep into your writing. Or let the environment and people around you be the source of your inspiration. I grew up in the Southwest United States and many of my screenplays take place in the heat of the desert and draw inspiration from the cultures around me. Even if you are writing a science fiction or fantasy script, you can use elements within your personal life to create a unique tale.

This is especially important if you plan to write a screenplay within 30 days because it cuts down on the time you need to research your topic before you begin. Most screenwriters will tell you that 50% of their jobs are researching for their scripts so they get a better understanding of the situations and characters they are developing. Starting out with a subject that you know personally can cut down on that time and make it easier for you jump right into the project. A feature film in 30 days can seem daunting but a screenplay is like a seed that you plant. It starts out small and expands into a finished script ready to film.

Take notes - Sometimes when you have an idea for a story things different scenes and ideas start flowing out. When you are struck with inspiration, write it down. Take notes on these ideas, whether it's just listing them out or writing them in prose, when the idea strikes you don't hesitate to grab some paper and

Start with one sentence – A Tagline is a one sentence description of the idea you have. It's a "hook", a catchphrase, something that is memorable and will leave your readers wanting more. It's a phrase that coveys the very foundation of your story in as few words as possible. Most of the time you'll find that taglines and advertising slogans are the same and used on movie posters, box covers, or in trailers or ads. Here is a classic example of a tagline from the movie **Alien**:

In space, no one can hear you scream.

This tagline works as a dramatic sentence that coveys the tone and the setting for that film and it paints a chilling scene for a space horror. Taglines are meant to supplement the title of the film and entice the audience to want to know more.

For your purposes, the tagline should be less about advertising your story and more about getting to the meat of it. Here is an example of a tagline for **My Super Ex-Girlfriend**:

He broke her heart. She broke his everything.

This tagline, while still catchy, hints at the dynamics of the two main characters and how they will interact with one another. It breaks down the story into simple terms and yet it's appealing enough to hook people into wanting more. Sometimes it's difficult to come up with the tagline until you have more of your idea fleshed out but it's always good to start with a hook that you can reference during your writing process.

Create a logline – The next step in the process is to create a one to two sentence summary of your script. This is the small description you would find when perusing through Netflix or on the TV guide channel. It breaks down the overall story of your script into simple wording and without giving away too much. Here is an example of a logline for the classic film, The Godfather:

The aging patriarch of an organized crime family hands over his empire to his reluctant youngest son. - IMDB.com

This logline explains the basic plot of the film and the overall goal of the main character. While the tagline is meant to tease the potential film viewer, the logline is meant to explain the basic plot so they know a little bit more about what they are going to see.

If you jotted down notes before when you were struck with inspiration, look over them again and come up with a basic one to two sentence description of what you want write.

Expand your Logline – Once you have a good logline for your idea and understand the basic plot, you will want to expand it into a **synopsis** that will be used as your base for the next steps in the process. A synopsis is a one paragraph description of the script that uses character names. This paragraph goes a little more into detail as far as your overall story. The synopsis should cover Who, What, When, Where, and Why. It should explain who your main characters are, what they are doing, when and where the story takes place, and a glimpse into why the characters are engaged in this story.

Let's take the logline from The Godfather and expand it into a synopsis:

This mob drama based in the late 1940's focuses on the powerful Italian-American crime family of Don Vito Corleone. When the aging Don refuses a proposition from a New York City drug dealer, Virgill Sollozzo it sparks a feud within the Italian mafia families that pulls in the Don's youngest son, Michael Corleone, into the violent world of syndicated crime. Although Michael tries to maintain a normal relationship with his wife, Kay he is drawn deeper into the family business, eventually assuming power from his aging father.

As you can see the synopsis builds on the logline of the aging patriarch who hands over control to his son but now the synopsis explains in more detail what is happening in the story.

The Tagline, Logline, and Synopsis should not take you very long to complete, especially if you have a strong concept rooted in what you know.

Total time for all three: **1-3 hours**

Chapter 2:
Easy Steps to Create the Outline

Once you have a good handle on your synopsis the next step is to create an outline of the major plot points that will occur in your story. Plot points are major events that happen in your story that move the main characters and your plot. Sometimes these events are decisions that the characters make, or they are outside forces that the characters are thrown into. Outlines are the skeleton of the script, they provide the structure in which your script will flow. The most common outline used to create a script is called the **3 Act Outline**.

Every story no matter what has to have a beginning, middle, and end and for most films this is done in 3 Acts. The 3 Act Outline is designed to help you figure out where your major events fall within the story. Below is a template that defines each section for this type of outline.

Act One: Day to Day life that suddenly changes

Set-up: Briefly explain the back story leading up to first major event that sets in motion the story. Sometimes this back story is part of the script, sometimes it is just simply referred to.

Inciting Incident: This is the trigger, the first event that happens that sets your characters in motion and starts the plot.

Plot Point: This is a smaller event that happens but it still affects the plot and continues it along.

Turning Point: This is a plot point where there is a twist in the story. Something changes and puts your character on a new path.

Act Two Turning Point: This is the plot turn that leads your character into Act Two. Usually this is a major event or decision that moves the characters into a whole new realm of possibilities.

Act Two: Down the Rabbit Hole

Plot Point: This is usually around the time that character is exploring the new "world." They are trying new things, meeting new characters or engaging in new activities.

Turning Point: This is usually around the time where the antagonist of the story is introduced and they throw a monkey wrench into the characters plans.

Act Three Turning Point – This turning point is usually when the hero has been captured or knocked down by the villain and is a low point for the main character.

Act Three: Final Showdown

Turning Point: This is usually when the main character decides to fight back against the villain and rises up to the challenge

Plot Point: This is usually when the main character plots how to defeat the villain and prepares themselves for "battle."

Climax: This is when the villain and the hero finally come face to face and the hero overpowers the villain in some way.

Resolution: The final outcome of the battle and the revelation of the main character and how they changed through their journey.

This outline is the most commonly used by screenwriters because it helps navigate the story for the writer to show the major conflict and who the protagonist and antagonist of the story are. I personally recommend when you write your outline to have at least 3 turning points and at 6 plot points within each Act. It may sound like a lot but when you begin to write everything out you will find that your story has many twists and turns and these plot points will help you stay on track.

There are other types of outlines that you can use if this doesn't seem to fit your style. Save the Cat by Blake Snyder is both a book and online website that is designed to help new writers develop their stories into screenplays. Save the Cat has it's own type of outline called a "Beat Sheet" that lists out the major plot points but also goes into the theme of the story and the goals and motivations of the characters. Save the Cat is a newer style of writing that has been embraced by the screenwriting community and I highly recommend viewing their website at www.savethecat.com.

Total Time to Write the Outline: **1 – 2 hours**

Chapter 3:
Developing your Characters

It's easy to overlook this step when you are bursting with inspiration and have created a solid outline, but this step is extremely important. Before you move on to the next step in the process you need to develop your characters and get to know them so that their journey is believable and they aren't just one dimensional characters with one goal and motivation. Truly great screenplays have characters that have complex emotions and motivations for the decisions that guide them through the story. One dimensional characters are very dull to watch on screen because their motivations and goals are shallow and lackluster. Think of your favorite film and your favorite character within it.

A simple and easy way to develop your characters is to create a Character Profile Sheet. These sheets are basic questions that you will answer for your character to give yourself a little more insight into them. These questions range from physical attributes to favorite things, and even to childhood memories or deep philosophical questions. The purpose of this is for you to get to know your character and be able to visualize them as you write your screenplay. The more you know about them, the easier is it to write their "voice" or rather their unique take on life. Here is an example of a condensed profile sheet that you can use:

Character Profile Sheet

Character Name:
Nickname:
Occupation:
Age/Birthday:
Weight/Height:
Hair color/cut:
Eye color:
Skin tone:
Personality Traits:
Good Habits:
Bad Habits:
Sense of Humor:
Passionate About:
Greatest Fear:
Optimist or Pessimist:
Introvert or Extrovert:
Cautious or Care Free:
Messy or Clean:
Type of Childhood:
Education:
Religion:
Economic Class:

Family Members:
Favorite Color:
Favorite Music:
Favorite Hobbies:
What would the character change about themselves:

This profile is the condensed down version of the profiles that I use for all of my characters. If you want to go more in depth you can touch upon deeper questions such as their outlook on life, or their thoughts on death or love. This step in the process is important however, it can be very time consuming so in the interest of saving on time, you should limit this to your main protagonist and antagonist for now. If you find that you have enough time, then create profiles for your supporting characters which will help you create strong dynamics.

Total Time to write Character Sheets for the Protagonist and Antagonist: **3-4 Hours**

Chapter 4:
Developing the story.

During the writing process sometimes you can get stuck. It happens to us all. We reach a point where we are so engrossed in the details of the characters or the plot that we lose focus on what the overall story can be. We miss the forest for the trees so to speak. Sometimes after developing your characters you'll find that the outline feels a bit weak, or that as you developed things, your outline has changed because your characters motivations or goals have changed and this has caused a wrench in your plans.

At times like this you want to pause and reflect on your overall story and how it affects your characters. It's one thing to have dynamic and interesting characters but if they don't have an equaling interesting journey to take, then your script can come off as uninspiring. Imagine if in the original Star Wars Luke Skywalker decided to stay home instead of go on his journey with Obi-Wan. Ask yourself: is your story pushing the limits of the your characters and what will they learn from their journey?

The Hero's Journey:

During the 20th century there was a new wave of exploring stories and how they come into creation. Renowned psychologists such as Carl Jung and Joseph Campbell began to see a pattern in all of the stories that have told throughout the ages. Stories shared similar archetypes and symbols which lead to the development of the *Hero's Journey* by Joseph Campbell. This book explains how all literature from ancient Greece up until now has a similar pattern for the main protagonist of the story. The 3 Act Outline that was detailed in Chapter 2 was based upon this Hero's Journey model but if you are having problems with some of your plot points in your outline, then I recommend referring back to the Hero's Journey to help flesh it out. Here is a brief outline of the Hero's Journey:

1. **The Ordinary World** – This is the daily life of the hero before the journey begins

2. **A Call to Adventure** – A major event forces the hero to consider going on this strange new journey.

3. **A Refusal to the Call** – The hero is conflicted about leaving his comfort zone to go into unknown territory

4. **Meeting of the Mentor** – The hero meets a wise sage that bestows upon him knowledge, skills, or equipment that will assist him in his journey

5. **Crossing the Threshold** - The hero leaves their comfort zone and heads into the unknown

6. **Tests, Allies, and Enemies** – The hero befriends new people and is faced with obstacles along the way.

7. **The Approach** – The hero and new formed allies hatch a plan to achieve the hero's goals.

8. **The Ordeal** – The hero s confronted with his worst fear or death and arises from it anew.

9. **The Reward** - The hero gains a treasure from facing his fears or death but the threat of losing the treasure to the villain is still at hand.

10. **The Road Back** – The hero is determined to defeat the villain in order to stop the threat of losing his new treasure.

11. **The Resurrection** – The hero is tested one last time and defeats the villain in order to restore balance to his homeland.

12. **Return Home** – The hero returns with the treasure in hand to a transformed life.

The Seven Basic Plots:

While the Hero's journey is a good launching pad, not all stories fall into the same plot lines. If you look at the story of Macbeth, and compare it to the film Cinderella, you will find that the protagonist of each is vastly different and their journeys don't seem to share any similarity. In 2004, Christopher Booker wrote the *Seven Basic Plots: Why we Tell Stories* which has helped writers categorize their stories and help achieve a certain purpose. Below are the 7 basic plots and a brief description for each:

Defeating the Monster – The protagonist goes head to head with the antagonist who threatens the family/homeland of the protagonist

Rags to Riches – A poor protagonist acquires wealth in the form of power, money, or love only to lose it again and regain after growing as a person.

The Quest – The protagonist sets out on a journey to acquire an important item, facing obstacles and temptations along the way.

Voyage and Return – The protagonist goes to a strange new land and experiences new things and returns with only the knowledge or experience from it.

Comedy – The protagonist overcomes a difficulty that results in a happy ending.

Tragedy - The protagonist becomes a villain after falling from grace to which his death is a happy ending.

Rebirth – The protagonist faces a major change in their preconceptions or ways after an event forces the change upon them.

When writing your outline, keep these plot lines in mind. Do you want your hero to become a villain and fall from grace, or do you want them to rise above their circumstance to gain wealth and fortune? These basic plots help drive a compelling story and can help you find focus when you are not sure what the next step in your hero's journey is going to be.

Total Time in Development: **1-2 hours**

Chapter 5:
Last Stop before the Script

The last step in the process before you begin to write the first draft of your screenplay is the treatment or a scene by scene breakdown. Let me preface that the terms "treatment" and "scene breakdowns" are kind of loose and interchangeable and vary depending who you talk to. From my professional experience my opinion is that a movie treatment is the marketing material used in the pitch package to sell the screenplay to potential investors or producers. A treatment for this purpose is generally 2-3 pages in length and is a short story prose version of the script. It highlights the major events and the characters of the story and touches lightly upon the characters goals and motivations. This type of treatment is meant to convey the script with brevity to people who have busy schedules and not enough time to read the script itself.

Treatment Format:

Treatments are written in a very specific format that makes it easy and fast to read. Generally they are written in Third person active present tense which allows them to be short and sweet.

When a character is introduced their name is spelled all in CAPS for the first time but regular for the remainder of the treatment. Here is a brief example of a properly formatted treatment:

JOHN, a hapless man who is down on his luck, finds a lottery ticket on the street. He thinks nothing of it until the winning numbers are announced and he discovers that he has won. John immediately cashes in the ticket only to discover that TERRY, a middle class businessman, is in fact the real buyer for the ticket. Terry sues John for the winning money and a battle between the two ensues.

Scene Breakdown:

A scene breakdown is sometimes referred to as a detailed treatment and can be anywhere from 5-10 pages in length. This scene breakdown is meant to help you visualize the script before you begin and can also be used by potential directors and producers to prepare for production as you complete the script. The scene breakdown is chronological list of every scene that will be in the script along with a brief description of what is going to happen in the scene. Typically the descriptions are 2-4 sentences in length unless you have a lot of action or heavy dialogue that occurs during that scene. The scene breakdown is written in the same tense as a treatment but will typically have a scene heading at the beginning of each new scene. Here is an example of a scene breakdown.

Scene 1: INT. COFFEE HOUSE – DAY

Shelly and Karen sit in the coffee house and discuss their plans for the weekend. Karen tells Sherry that she is going on a blind date later that evening.

Scene 2: INT. KARENS HOUSE – EVENING

Karen prepares for her date as she puts makeup on in the bathroom. She hears a crack of thunder outside her window and contemplates canceling the date.

Scene 3: EXT. RAINY STREETS – NIGHT

Karen rushes through the wet streets with an umbrella in hand. Suddenly her umbrella is swept away by the rain and she gets soaked.

Scene 4: INT. RESTAURANT – NIGHT

Karen sits at the table soaked to the bone, her makeup completely ruined. Her blind date approaches her at the table. Karen looks up to see that her date is completely soaked by the rain as well and holds a dripping bouquet of flowers. Karen smiles and laughs.

The scene headings represent whether the scene takes place inside (Interior or INT) or outside (Exterior EXT) and the location and time of day. These scene headings will be used again in the actual script and help the director and producer plan their locations for filming.

A scene breakdown can sometimes take much longer if you are writing a movie with a lot of scenes and characters. In the effort to save on time, try to limit your scene locations and characters or skip this step if you are already behind schedule in your writing process. This step does help when writing the script but some writers, like myself for example, can visually see the scenes play out in their heads and this step tends to bog down the process.

Total Time for a Treatment: **1-2 hours**

Total Time for a Scene Breakdown: **4-5 hours**

Chapter 6:
Plan it Out

Writing a screenplay in 30 days is no easy feat. Sometimes it can take months or even years for a screenwriter to produce to a script that is ready to pitch. If you aren't careful you can fall into the trap that many new writers have; getting so wrapped up in the pre-planning that you never actually write the script. The key is to plan out your time. Sometimes inspiration hits and it's easy and fast to get a lot of work done but when writers block hits it feels like there is no end in sight. Here are some ways that you can stay on track with your screenplay and plan ahead so you can meet that 30 day deadline.

Schedule Writing Time:

This may seem simple but sometimes it's the basic things that help us get things accomplished. If you are like me, you probably are already balancing a busy schedule of work, family, projects, and the general day to day of living life. The hardest part about taking on a new project like writing a screenplay is devoting enough time to get it done. So the first step is to pencil in your calendar designated writing times. It can be a few times a week, even just for a an hour at a time but you need to allocate yourself enough time to get it done. Start by looking through your calendar and seeing where you have available spots. Based on your current schedule, including general life maintenance, calculate the maximum amount of available free time you have to devote to this project. You may not need the maximum amount but it is helpful for you to know this when setting your pace.

Find Your Pace:

Every writer has a different pace to which they write. For some writers a simple paragraph can take them hours, for others its a matter of minutes. Before you allocate time for this project you need to know what kind of pace you can work in comfortably in order to meet that 30 day deadline. One way you can do this is to write out a 1 page scene and time yourself while you write. Then calculate the time it took you times the number of pages you want to approximately write. Most feature length scripts are anywhere from 90 to 120 pages, so if one page took you 15 minutes to type then 90 pages will take you 1350 minutes or approximately 22 hours. That seems like a lot of time but spread out over three weeks and you are looking about 5-7 hours per week.

For me personally, I can type about 5 pages an hour which is one page every 12 minutes. So based on my approximate time, in order for me to complete a 90 page script it will take me a total of 18 hours to complete. Now this is just based on my page count, there are many varying factors that go into the process such as writers block or an external event comes up . You need to allocate yourself enough wiggle room that if you do have writers block or there is a reason you can't sit down to write that day, you still have enough time to complete the script within 30 days.

Average Schedule Time: To write a screenplay in 30 days here is a good average pace and schedule that you can use.

Week One: Pre-Script Material

This week includes the tagline, logline, synopsis, outline, character profiles, and treatment. Each of these items will vary in time but you should be able to complete everything within 10 hours of work, or 1.5 hours a day.

Week Two: Half of the First Draft

This week based on your writing pace you should be able to complete the first half of your screenplay up to page 45. Generally this is about

12 hours of work (based on approximately 4 pages an hour, or half a page every 15 minutes.)

Week Three: The Second Half of the First Draft

This week you will complete the first draft of the script based on the same pace you went the previous week. 12 hours per week sounds like a lot of time to devote but it breaks down to about an hour and a half per day. This is about the same amount of time that most people spend watching TV per week, so if you replace your nightly viewing with your writing you will be well on track to completing your script.

Week Four: Revisions and Final Draft

I recommend that after you finish the first draft you give yourself a couple of days to step away from the script and then review it again with fresh eyes. When you pick it back up you want to review it as if you were reading it for the first time. From there you can catch plot holes or inconsistencies to fix for your final draft. At this time you will also go through and make sure you don't have any spelling or grammatical issues and your formatting is correct with industry standards. Approximate time for this is anywhere from 5-10 hours.

Conclusion

Thank you again for purchasing this book!

I hope this book was able to help you to get started on your journey to crafting your screenplay in 30 days. The creative process can be trying but with persistence planning you can be on your way to completing that story that have been burning inside you.

The next step is to write the first draft of the script which is outlined in the next book of this series.

Finally, if you enjoyed this book, then I'd like to ask you for a favor, would you be kind enough to leave a review for this book on Amazon? It'd be greatly appreciated!

Please leave a review for this book on Amazon!

Thank you and good luck!

Book II
The 30-Day Screenplay Challenge

Writing a successful screenplay in a month
– a step-by-step guide

By George Lucas

Introduction

I want to thank you and congratulate you for purchasing the book, *"The 30-Day Screenplay Challenge"*.

This book contains proven steps and strategies on how to write a well-constructed and professionally formatted screenplay in just 30 days.

Starting off with a compact overview on the most important things to know about screenwriting, this book heads off to give you a comprehensive step-by-step guide with work instructions for each of the 30 days. You will learn what to keep track of, you will join the challenge and in the end, you will hold your own professional screenplay in your hands.

Thanks again for purchasing this book, I hope you enjoy it!

Screenplay Writing
– Some Thoughts for the Beginning

It happens to pretty much every one of us: We go to the movies, we are all excited about the film, but when it finally starts – we are disappointed. At least, we leave the cinema with the good knowledge that we could have written a much better screenplay, but then, we never do it. Maybe because we think it is never going to sell, or because we are not a professional, or even just because our language teacher in 5th grade told us to never take a job in writing. However, writing and possibly even selling a screenplay is a dream that not only those living close to Hollywood dream.

For many, the main reason not to start writing is time. We are all wrapped up in our everyday work and family life, and finding the time to just sit down and write can seem an impossible task, especially when the goal of holding a finished screenplay in ones hands is months, if not a year, away. This is where this book comes in, because I dare you to write a professional screenplay in no more than 30 days. You may deem this impossible, but think about it – some of the biggest screenplay writers out there swear on getting the main part of a screenplay down in less than a week. If they can do it, you can too, especially since you now got this guide at your hands.

The advantages of getting your screenplay down within such short time are obvious, one being that knowing your goal is just a month away will help you to really stay focused. Additionally, you do not spend a lot of time on a screenplay without knowing if it is actually going to sell, which will probably be your goal after you finished writing. This makes joining the challenge a great opportunity not just for hobby writers, but for professionals, too. Ever spent months on a screenplay you really believed in, just to still have it sitting in your drawer to this day? Ever encountered a writing block because of all the distractions that drew your attention from writing? Those situations are hard on writers, the more so because their livelihood depends on getting their work out.

If anything, after this month you will be able to say that you actually did something that even many of the most professional writers never managed to, which will be a boost to your confidence and highlight your skills as a writer in a way that sticks out.

Get Prepared

Before starting the 30-Day Screenplay Challenge, it is crucial that you take the right measures to get properly prepared for the task. Imagine yourself like a runner right before an important sprint. You will want to get warmed up and stretched in order to go the full distance at maximum speed.

It is important that you get familiar with some basic concepts and ideas on writing a screenplay. To make it easier for you, I want to give an overview on the most important things.

Basic rules for writing and formatting a screenplay

The most important thing to internalize before you start writing is as simple as it is crucial: Write visually. A screenplay, unlike a novel or a short story, is not meant to be *read* it is meant to be *seen*. If the visuals you create in your screenplay are not drawing the reader in, the visuals on screen will likely not do it either. Always strive for strong images. In order to accomplish that, there are a few basic concepts that will help you:

- Let characters unfold themselves: You may be tempted to excessively use the descriptions of scenes and characters to give a detailed idea on where your characters come from and who they are. The simple truth though is that this is not going to get your point across. Your characters need to unfold their backstory and persona by their actions and dialogue. Let characters tell about themselves, instead of you telling something about them.

- Keep action lines short: Not just for the above reason, you should try to keep your action lines as short as possible. As a basic rule, a paragraph of action line should not exceed three lines of text. A good screenplay, on average, has action line paragraphs of two lines or less throughout the majority of the screenplay.

- Write in present tense: If you pitch your screenplay to someone, or even if you never will, it should read dynamically, transporting the future movie as good as possible. Therefore, always use present tense, as it will keep your action lines and story vivid and forward.

As important as the writing style is for the success of your screenplay, as important is choosing the correct format. It is a good idea to catch a look at some successful screenplays before starting on your own, as you will quickly get not just a good idea of narrative style but also of formatting. Get used to the following elements of a screenplay:

- The slugline: This is a line of text, always written in CAPS, that appears at the beginning of each new scene and describes the setting, especially location and time. Common abbreviations to describe the location are INT., meaning the interior of a setting, and EXT., meaning the exterior of that setting. An example is INT. CAFÉ BAR, where you would see the characters appear inside of a bar, or EXT. CAFÉ BAR, where they would be standing outside of the bar.

- The transition: As you are writing visually, you will have to give an idea on how the current scene ends and the next scene starts. Common transitions are FADE IN / FADE OUT, where scenes are gradually faded in and out. If you want a harsh cut, you use CUT TO at the end of the scene. If you want scenes to fade into each other, you use the term DISSOLVE TO.

- Special shots: Maybe you have a scene in mind where the camera is meant to do something particular. If you want that to be captured on screen, you need to write it down. One of the most common terms for special camera shots is CLOSE UP, always with a description of what person or object should be filmed from near, like "CLOSE UP on the photo in Anna's hand". When putting FREEZE FRAME, the image on screen will stop and become an inanimate photo. If you want to show that a large portion of time is passing, you will usually use MONTAGE to describe the images the viewer is going to see to transport the message of what happens in a big span of time within just a few seconds. Sometimes on screen, you can see a camera following a person without actually being mounted on a tripod but freely moving with the camera operator, such a shot is indicated by the term TRACKING SHOT.

- Things that happen in the background or off-screen: If you describe things that happen in the background, abbreviate background to *b.g.* If you want a character's voice to speak from a position off-screen but still within the action, you use the term O.S. If the character, on the other hand, is supposed to speak from the off or narrate over a scene, you use V.O., which stands for "Voice Over".

Tools and instruments you need and arranging your workspace

Just like the runner will not just need to warm up and get stretched but also needs the right shoes to conclude a run, you need the right working space with proper tools. They do not necessarily have to be expensive, it is more important that you arrange them in a way that ideally supports your workflow and allows to minimize all distractions. The list of instruments and things you should prepare includes:

- An easy-to-use computer or laptop: Choose a model you are familiar with and like working on, as it will make it easier to get a lot of work done in little time. Make sure the keyboard is comfortable for you to use. Tidy your desktop and hard-drive beforehand, and delete or move all files that could possibly distract you from working. Create neatly organized folders for your screenplay project.

- Paper and pen or pencil: Believe it or not, you will want to use paper and pen from time to time.

- Word-processing software: The choice of software you use for writing depends both on your budget and taste. Basically, you can write a screenplay using a simple word-processing program. This takes some time formatting properly, which is why some people prefer to use screenwriting software. Make sure you also have access to software that corrects your grammar and spelling.

- A printer: Working on the computer is fine, but you will see how much easier proofreading can go when you have your script black on white in front of you.

Arrange your tools and workspace in a way that is helpful to you. Everything you need, from the pen and paper to your favorite comfort food for stressful moments, should be available at your fingertips. Every time you have to get up will interrupt your flow, let alone if you have to start searching for things. Minimize distractions by eliminating things that you know will have that power over you. Can't go without checking your emails or social media profiles once an hour? Switch off your internet. Don't know how to tell your grandmother you can not speak to her right now? Unplug the phone. Disconnect, turn off and lock up whatever it is that will make this project hard to finish.

The 30-Day Screenplay Challenge
Part I: Develop your Story

So, you made all the necessary preparations, you told your friends you are out of town for the next month and you stocked up on coffee and snacks: You are good to go. Let's get you started with the 30-Day Screenplay Challenge!

The challenge will be divided into four sections, each leading you to an important step to finishing your screenplay. In the first part of the challenge, you will develop your overall story, get to know your hero or heroine and find a single sentence that perfectly describes the essence of your story.

When developing your story, keep in mind that everything you will be writing about later is meant to be visually strong and mainly transported through dialogue. Go for story ideas that scream for awesome visuals and for which you can actually see captivating scenes in your mind's eye. Make sure your idea can be formed into a plot that holds enough drama to build a proper arc of suspense with a thrilling climax. This may seem unimportant if you are not going for a thriller or horror movie, but even romantic comedy needs that dramatic line of action that leads to the characters nearly crashing before they can be happy ever after.

Day 1: Brainstorm away

The aim of day 1 is to leave you with a small set of different story ideas that you can work on. While it may be true that it is hard to force creativity, you can use brainstorming techniques to effectively come up with a hand full of good stories in a day. At this stage, nothing needs to be finished or well-constructed yet, two or three sentences that describe the main purpose of the plot are fine.

You probably did think about awesome ideas for a screenplay before, so start by writing down those ideas. Do not end here though, not even if you think you already found your story – you may never know what is lurking just around the corner of your imagination. Go on by using different techniques that can help you come up with more ideas:

- Take your favorite genre of film and come up with an idea that ideally fits that genre. If you have trouble finding ideas, let yourself be inspired by your favorite movies or characters and what makes them unique.

- Draw from your own experiences. Sometimes, life brings us stories that no one could make up. A good idea can also be to think of how you saw the world as a child, or dreams that maybe haunted you at some point.

- Write about something you are passionate about. Whether you love base-jumping or swimming, it will be easier for you to write about things you love and are familiar with. The same goes for feelings. If you do not know what losing your big love feels like, it might not be a good idea to write about that.

Day 2: Identify your Story

On day 2, you will go through the stories you came up with the day before and choose the one story you will continue to work on. Make a pre-selection by feeling. If a story does not seem like something you will enjoy writing – kick it. You need to be passionate and excited about writing it. Narrow your set of stories down to those you really believe in. Between those, choose by asking some practical questions:

- Is there enough potential for drama and action to fill a feature length film and keep the viewers engaged?

- Does the story provide characters which will stand out and be strong on camera?

- How big is the potential for strong scenes and visuals?

- Can the main portion of the story be told through actions or dialogue?

Go through those questions for each of the ideas left. In the end, decide for the one you consider most promising.

Day 3: Create your Hero

A strong movie stands or falls by a convincing protagonist. Even if you may not want to call him or her that, your protagonist needs to be a hero or heroine.

At this stage, it is not important yet what your main character will be called or what he or she exactly looks like. It can help you though to create a work name and imagine your protagonist in as many details as possible. Make him or her vivid to yourself – let them become a breathing human being. Now think about where that person comes from, what they experienced before the story line begins and what is important to them. Make clear to yourself what role the character will be playing in the movie and what he or she is meant to go through. Try to write everything down as detailed as you can.

Day 4: Write your Log Line

With your story chosen and your hero called to life, you are ready to lay the foundations for your plot. The most important parts every movie has is the protagonist, the antagonist and a goal. Think about your hero, what is his or her goal? There has to be something he or she wants to achieve throughout the course of the movie. What other characters are important as accomplices of the protagonist? Write your characters down on a sheet of paper and draw lines between them to indicate their relationships.

If you found out what your hero wants and who helps them in getting there, think about the antagonist. That does not necessarily have to be a person, even though often, it will be. The antagonist could as well be an institution or a situation though. But find that one person or thing that is most opposed to your protagonist, and then develop it as detailed as you did develop your hero. In the end, ask yourself whether there are any important characters you forgot, and put them onto your map of people.

Once you finished those steps, you will have a very clear idea of what your story will be about. Now you can write your log line. In professional movie and screenwriting business, the log line is a one-sentence synopsis of the plot used for marketing purposes. Screenwriters use it to pitch their newest screenplay to producers within one sentence. Even if you do not plan on doing that, writing your log line before you actually start writing your screenplay gives yourself an idea and direction. Whenever you feel like you are losing your leitmotif or getting lost in details, look at the log line and it will get you back on track.

A perfect log line is short and to the point, and contains all three important elements of your story: The protagonist, the antagonist and the goal. Do not mention names, keep it simple. The log line of a romantic comedy could be "'A woman falls in love with her dentist and has to run against his attractive receptionist to win his heart."

The 30-Day Screenplay Challenge
Part II: Get your Story Organized

Now you got your story laid out in front of you, you will probably want to start writing straight away. You will need to take a few more days of preparation though. That will help you to write your story in a way and structure that is appropriate for filming and cinema.

In this phase, you will finally work out the particular scenes and important visuals for your screenplay. From now on, it is important to keep in mind that your story is supposed to have an arc of suspense and that the main plot has to revolve around the protagonist and the other main characters striving to achieve their goal. With that in mind, you can now sculpture your rough story into a proper outline.

Day 5: Write a Treatment

If you ever before had a chance to get a view into the world of screenwriting and movie business, you will probably know that a treatment is extremely important in getting your screenplay sold. Basically, the treatment is a synopsis of your movie idea in 2 two 5 pages and contains all important elements, characters and twists of the story. Because it is such a comprehensive preview, it is a powerful tool not just for selling but also for writing your screenplay. As with the log line, the treatment nails down your story and is something that can get you back on track whenever you get lost.

Sit down and carefully look through the materials you crafted the days before. Develop the rough outline of your story and how things are going to evolve. You do not need to be sure on what part will take up which amount of the film or come up with any particular scenes yet. But craft the overall plot in a way that it can be told in a few pages.

When writing your treatment, start with the title. The title may still change in the future, but having a work title is important. Put it on top of your treatment. Then follow with the log line. After that, write down a synopsis of your story, introducing all important characters and circumstances and giving all important aspects and twists of the plot.

Day 6: Build a Structure

Based on your treatment, you can start developing your story in all details. In order to do that, it is good to get familiar with the general structure every screenplay should have. There are 5 elements that follow each other in a fixed order:

- Inciting Incident: This describes the first part of the screenplay, in which characters are introduced, their initial situations are shown and then a key event happens that kicks off the events to come.

- Struggle: Once the inciting incident occurred, your characters will need to struggle against different forces in order to achieve their goals.

- Crisis: As a good movie lives off a thrilling plot, it is necessary that your characters head towards a growing crisis to unfold the drama.

- Climax: The climax usually only makes up a small portion of the screenplay, but is the point of highest tension within the script.

- Resolution: After the climax, the suspension you built up will be broken by offering how the crisis will be stopped. This does not necessarily mean a happy ending.

Take a big sheet of paper and draw an arc of suspension onto it that represents the upper model. It is important to get the relations right: The "Inciting Incident" part should take up a quarter of your sheet, "Struggle" and "Crisis" together amount for half of it, and then "Climax" and "Resolution" make for the missing quarter.

Go through your treatment and map your story out onto the sheet, determining which parts belong into what section of the arc of suspension. When you got everything in, think of scenes or details to the story that accompany them well and write them down where they belong. That way, you get a more detailed idea and plot outline to build on in the next few days.

Day 7: Create your Scenes

Today is the day when your screenplay will actually come to life – today, you will develop all scenes of the movie. You do not have to write them yet, the purpose of day 7 is to divide your plot into all scenes necessary for the screenplay.

A feature length screenplay has around 50 to 70 scenes. Take your arc of suspense from the day before and count how many scenes you already got. Those will probably be the key actions to your storyline, but now you have to build a narrative around them. Close your eyes, and imagine yourself in a cinema. What will your movie start like? Write it down, in just as much detail as necessary for you to be able to recall it the next day. Go on like this, always keep your eye on your arc of suspense and your treatment. Build all scenes like that, but resist the urge to already write them. A few words can be enough to nail down what you have in mind, then move on to the next scene.

Make sure that the number of scenes you create again correlates to the scheme of 25 % inciting incident, 50 % struggle and crisis and 25 % climax and resolution. If you find that hard, write all scenes right onto the arc of suspense, that way you keep the whole picture in mind.

Days 8 and 9: Get the Details Right

On the following two days, go through each scene of your future movie and write a synopsis of what happens. Again, you do not need to write proper dialogue or actions yet, but you should nail down the details of what happens in each scene and what the characters will be talking about. Also think of making useful connections between the scenes, working out how the characters got where they are from where they just came. If you find that scenes are missing or misplaced, add new scenes and delete or move existing ones. At the end of day 9, you will have crafted what is called a script outline, the framework for writing your screenplay.

The 30-Day Screenplay Challenge
Part III: Write your Story

After all the preparation and story building you did in the last 9 days, you are now ready to properly write down your screenplay. It is common practice to start with what is called a flash draft. The flash draft basically is the first version of your screenplay, but what is special to it is the way you write it. You do not tweak words or look back to see if your grammar got out of order. You just *write*, as quick as you can. Let your creativity flow, and keep interruptions as little as possible.

Days 10 to 16: Write your Flash Draft

To just sit down and write is something that other people than you can do little to prepare you for. In the next 7 days, it is more crucial than in all the days before or after that you focus on your work and do not allow distractions to appear. Do not think twice about what you just wrote, just continue writing as the words form in your mind. Do not correct grammar or unlucky wordings. Everything that matters now is that you get your story out in those few days.

When you start your day, it is a good idea to have a quick look at where you left off yesterday, in order to tie in perfectly with the last scene written. Only read back the last paragraph written though. If you encounter writing blocks, do not read back but allow yourself to have a little break. Have a cup of coffee, go for a walk in the sun or have a quick shower. Do something that enables your mind to switch off and regenerate. Watching TV or reading a book will not do the job. Instead, do something that makes you feel at peace. Go back to your workspace after a pre-defined period of time.

At the end of the day, look through the following checklist to make sure you are on the right track with your work. If you find there is trouble, do not correct things straight away. Instead, take notes for later revision or to keep in mind the next day. Things you should check every evening are:

- Did I write the appropriate number of scenes and / or pages to achieve my goal?

- Is my plot even, or does it seem like there are scenes missing or misplaced?

- Do my characters unfold well or do they seem distant and mysterious?

- Are my characters and plot authentic, or do they come across unreal?

- Did I stick to my arc of suspense and the inciting-incident-struggle-crisis-climax-resolution-model?

- Is my story consistent with my log line, treatment and script outline?

The 30-Day Screenplay Challenge
Part IV: Revise your Screenplay

Once you got your flash draft finished, you may feel like the main part of the work has been done, but the biggest portion of your work is only about to start now. A professional screenplay needs to be accurately proofread and formatted and polished in its narrative to make it shine like gold. In order to do this effectively, you will divide the two areas of speech and format and work on them separately.

It is especially important now that you keep an eye on your log line and treatment and make sure your story is consistent with what you want to tell. Make sure that your sluglines and action lines draw vivid, meaningful images.

Days 17 to 21: Revise your Story

Your revision work starts off with revising your actual story. For those few days, you do not need to look at the format of the screenplay yet, instead make sure your plot comes out at its best. Go from scene to scene and keep an eye on the following points:

- Grammar and spelling mistakes: A good screenplay needs proper grammar and spelling. Do not be ashamed to use correction software, even the best writers do it.

- Visual writing: As you read through the scenes, let them play on a screen in your mind's eye. If you can not imagine them on screen or they seem boring, rewrite them.

- Short dialogue and action lines: Sometimes, a long monologue by the hero is fine, but in general, try to keep your dialogue to three lines or less per pronouncement. The same goes, as already explained, for action lines. That way, you make sure your story moves quick enough.

- Natural characters: Make sure the language of your characters comes across natural and that they behave authentically. Their statements and actions should correspond with their background.

- Thrilling scenes: A rule in screenwriting is to enter a scene late and leave it early. If you are satisfied with a scene, strike out the first and last sentence. If you feel the scene definitely needs them to be understandable, put them back in. If you feel that is not the case, leave them out and go on until you find the scene has been narrowed down to what is really necessary.

- Structure: Make sure the length of your screenplay is appropriate – a feature length screenplay has 100 to 120 pages – and corresponds to the structure of 25 % inciting incident, 50 % struggle and crisis and 25 % climax and resolution.

Days 22 to 26: Get your Format Straight

Correct all formatting mistakes. The following checklist will help you to examine each scene:

- Is there a proper slugline in all CAPS explaining the setting?

- Did I make remarks where characters are meant to speak from the off or the background?

- Have I used terms that indicate special camera shots?

- Did I indicate what transitions to use?

Day 27: Read out Loud

Day 27 starts with a printer – print out your screenplay and stitch it together. Now sit down somewhere you feel comfortable doing so and start reading your screenplay loudly. This may at first seem weird to you. If you wish, it can be a good idea to not just read but play the scenes somewhat for yourself. That way, you will identify things that do not sound as good spoken as they did when you wrote them. Make notes within your screenplay whenever you encounter such situations.

Day 28: Get your Story Ready for Screen

Now you can eliminate the last mistakes. Sit down with your printed screenplay and the notes you made the day before and correct all scenes that still need work to make them sound more natural. Read them out loud directly again, to see if they sound better now.

Day 29: Group Up

This could possibly be the hardest task to you, but it is as well an important one. Every screenplay writer should test their screenplay in a small setting. Therefore, invite some friends or family members you respect and trust and have a roundtable readout with them. Such a readout is usually done by film crews and actors before the actual filming starts, but now you will use that technique to see how others react to your story. Make sure everyone invited has a copy of the latest version of your screenplay. Assign parts to different people, and then read or play the screenplay together. Ask them to give an honest feedback on what they liked and did not like.

Day 30: Finalize your Screenplay

With the knowledge you gathered the day before, sit down once more and contemplate whether there is anything you feel you should change. Make sure to not let yourself be confused though. Tastes are different, and not everyone will be over the moon with your screenplay. Rather try to work out whether you can see parallels in the feedback given to you. If all of your friends except for one loved your protagonist, you probably do not have to change anything. If they all considered him arrogant and distant though, go through your screenplay and see how you can fix this problem.

Congratulations!

You made it! It is probably in order to celebrate now. You have gone through a nerve-wrecking but exciting 30 days that probably left you entirely desperate more than once but also boosted your confidence and proved your skills as a writer. You have learnt the elements a successful screenplay consists of and how to use all rules of format and language to polish your result to the best end product you could have made.

Once the excitement and happiness wears off, you will probably start wondering what to do with your screenplay now. And whether you were planning on it from the first moment of writing on or not, you will want to sell your screenplay. That is a major task to load upon yourself, but in the next part of this series, you will learn 3 different strategies on how to make money from the screenplay you just wrote.

Conclusion

Thank you again for purchasing this book!

I hope this book was able to help you to write a screenplay in as little time as possible.

The next step is to make money from the screenplay you wrote.

Finally, if you enjoyed this book, then I'd like to ask you for a favor, would you be kind enough to leave a review for this book on Amazon? It'd be greatly appreciated!

Please leave a review for this book on Amazon!

Thank you and good luck!

Book III
30 Day Screenplay Challenge

How to Write the Script

By George Lucas

Introduction

I want to thank you and congratulate you for downloading the book, *"insert book title here"*.

This book contains proven steps and strategies on how to write an industry standard screenplay with the proper formatting, tips on creating dynamic characters and scenes, and common mistakes and traps that new writers can fall into.

I am a professional script editor and have worked on hundreds of screenplays throughout the years. This book will help you understand how to create good screenplay formatting to help propel your story into new heights.

Thanks again for downloading this book, I hope you enjoy it!

Chapter 1:
Screenplays Versus Novels

As a screenwriter and script editor the hardest part of my job is explaining it to novel authors. Most authors who write prose books both fiction and non fiction have difficulty understanding how a screenplay works and some even discredit screenwriting as a lesser form of literature. But just because those authors cannot fathom the complexity of screenwriting does not mean screenplays are any less dynamic, emotional, and engaging as traditional prose. Screenplays are a look into a story from the outside in and are an incredible form of writing all in their own. A good screenplay can move it's reader and can be the foundation for cinematic masterpiece.

Screenplay format is very different from prose format for good reasons. In screenwriting you want to convey the story in measured words. Typical feature length screenplays are between 90 to 120 pages and each page of a script translates to roughly one minute of screen time. So a 90 minute movie typically hails from a 90 page screenplay. When you only have a certain amount of pages to work with but have a complicated story to tell, you need to use your words carefully. In a novel, it's easy to get lost in the details, the descriptive settings, the deep inner emotions of the characters, all can be explored when you have an unlimited number of pages. Just look at classics such as Moby Dick which has 396 pages. Something that immense could never work in screenwriting, it would be 396 minutes long and people would walk out of the theater before the film is complete.

Screenwriting is a more precise style of writing. It doesn't elaborate on the details, it cuts to the chase and emphasizes a visual medium. When I write a screenplay, I visualize how it would look on the big screen and base my writing around that. Sometimes I will have the entire movie laid out in my mind before I begin the script. Novels are written from the inside looking out: it is a perspective of a character or group of characters and how they interact. Screenplays are written from the outside looking in: They are written as if an audience is watching the group of characters interact.

Differences Between the Two

Tense Matters: Novels can be written in various tenses and from various perspectives . They can be written in first, second, or third person and can be past tense, present tense, or even future tense. They can be written in active or passive form, they can even be written in broken sentences. In screenwriting there is only ONE type of tense and form that is used - Third Person, Active Present Tense. This will be explored more further in the book.

No Internal Dialogue: A common use in novel writing is the use of internal dialogue. This is the internal thoughts of a character and how the feel about a situation. In screenwriting there is no room for internal dialogue and the visual aspect must be kept in mind at all times. There is way to show internal thoughts on screen but the general use of internal dialogue in a novel is not done in screenwriting.

Page Format: You have probably seen examples of screenplays and noticed that the page format is much different that a regular book. The spacing on the pages for each of the different parts of the script are important because it makes it easy to follow for the production team as they film the scenes. In a typical script the spacing is as follows:

1. 1.5 left margin

2. 12 point Courier font

3. 1 inch right margin

4. 1 inch top and bottom margins

5. Dialogue is 2.5 inches from the left side of the page

6. Page numbers are at the top right corner. Title pages do not count as a page of the script therefore the page numbers should start at 1 after it.

As you read through this book, I will go more in depth on the page layout but these are the basics to follow.

Sections of the Script: There are several components to a script and each play a vital role.

– Scene Headings: Often these are referred to as "Slug-lines" and they set up the location and time of day in which the scene takes place.

– Narrative (Action) Descriptions: This section describes the visual action that is unfolding on the screen.

– Character Cue: The cue for a characters lines of dialogue

– Dialogue: What the characters actually say

- Parentheticals: The way a character says their lines

- Transitions: A break between scenes, generally used by the editor to cut the scenes together.

Chapter 2:
Setting Up Your World

– When you sit down to write a screenplay, you want to convey the setting in which your characters are interacting. The world that you build around your characters is important because it helps visualize the story and brings it to life. Building the setting starts with the Scene Headings and is elaborated within the Narrative Descriptions.

– Scene Headings

– When start a scene you always begin with the scene heading. The scene heading tells the reader if the setting is indoors or outdoors, the scene location, and the time of day. Scene Headings have a very specific format. It is in all capitalization and always starts with either INT. (interior) or EXT. (exterior) followed by the location then a space and dash followed by the time of day. Here is an example of a properly formatted scene heading:

- INT. LIVING ROOM – DAY

- If you have a location such as as a house with multiple scenes in different rooms you can add in an extra detail within the location section such as:

- INT. JOHN'S HOUSE – LIVING ROOM – DAY

- If you have characters that are moving from one room to another within the same location your scene heading can be shortened down to just the location. Here is an example:

- INT. JOHN'S HOUSE – BATHROOM – DAY

- John brushes his teeth and then leaves.

- BEDROOM

- John enters the bedroom and gets dressed.

- This only works for scene headings that are within the same location and do not move from inside to outside or vice versa.

– For the time of day there are several options you can use. For a generic time you can use DAY or NIGHT. If it's more specific you can use MORNING, AFTERNOON, EVENING, DUSK, etc. However unless is it a vital part of your story refrain from using specific time such as 12:30pm.

– Another type of time that you can use is either CONTINUOUS or SAME. "Continuous" is used if you have established the time of day in a previous scene and the following scene is a continuation of that same scene but moved into a different location. "Same" refers to a scene that takes place in a different location but at the same time as the previous scene. Here are two examples:

– INT. LIVING ROOM – DAY

– John hears the doorbell ring. He walks to the door.

– EXT. FRONT DOOR – CONTINUOUS

– Amanda stands at the front door. John opens the door.

- INT. LIVING ROOM – DAY

- John sits in his living room and reads.

- EXT. DRIVE WAY - SAME

- Amanda pulls up into the driveway and gets out.

- So while the first example shows a continuation of the sequence of events, the second shows that two different sequences of events are occurring at the same time.

- If you have a scene that is a flashback or a dream sequence, you'll want to add in a note after the time of day. For example:

- INT. LIVING ROOM – DAY: FLASHBACK

- Once you have added that into your scene heading there is no need to add it in the narrative descriptions or transitions.

- If you are writing a film that takes place in space or in a location where there is no real time of day to reference, then you can either leave the time of day blank or add in a reference to the timelessness of the location:

- INT. SPACE STATION – SPACE

- Scene Headings are a vital step in the process as they are a quick guide for the production team to know where they need to shoot for each scene. In a production draft of a script you will find Scene numbers or markers that indicate the scene within the script. For a screenplay in which you are trying to sell, scene numbers are not needed.

- **Narrative Descriptions**

- This section of the screenplay describes the setting and the actions of the scene. This can be the hardest part of screenwriting for some as these descriptions need to be precise while still creating a visual image of the scene. Narrative descriptions need to convey the visual element of the script in measured words. Because of this, narrative descriptions are done in a very specific perspective, tense, and form.

- Where novels have the freedom to write in various perspectives, 1st person through 3rd person, screenplays are always written in **3rd person omnipotent.** This perspective allows for the script to be read as if it is an audience looking in on the story. The screenwriter is telling the story

- Here is an example of the correct narrative descriptive format:

- *Jenny walks into the store and stops. She turns and looks at Peter. Jenny and Peter smile at one another.*

- The most common mistake that new screenwriters do is write in passive present tense or in past active tense. Here is an example of both below:

- **Passive Present Tense** – *Jenny is walking into the store and the begins to stop. She begins to turn and is looking over at Peter. Jenny and Peter are smiling at one another.*

- **Active Past Tense** – *Jenny walked into the store and stopped. She turned and looked at Peter. Jenny and Peter smiled at one another.*

- Both of these styles of writing are incorrect for screenplays because they take up so much space on the page. Where the active present tense takes up only 20 words on the page, the passive tense takes up 29 words. It may not seem like a big difference but as you write the screenplay you will discover that it adds up quickly. As a script editor I come across this issue often and one script in particular that I edited was written completely in passive present tense. After revising all of the action descriptions to active present tense, the screenplay went from 95 pages in length down to 65, which is a huge difference.

- **Create a good visual**

- Once you have created your scene headings and understand the correct tense for the narrative descriptions you want to create an engaging visual world for your reader. You want to include details that will help they see the characters and the settings.

- **Describe the action:** If your scene has a choreographed fight within it, don't just say that the characters fight. Describe how they are fighting. The description needs to keep visual an engaging but leave enough room for the reader to use their imaginations.

- **Create Establishing Scenes:** Many times in a film you will see the outside of a building prior to the scene inside unfolding. When establishing a new settings sometimes it's good to write in what is often called an establishing shot. This is a shot of the exterior of the location so the audience can get a good sense of where the scene takes place. If your two characters are located in a Parisian cafe, then you may want to describe a scene of the Paris cityscape before you begin the scene. This description can be brief but it allows the reader to get a good sense of where everything is.

- **Keep it External:** Many times writers will get caught up in the details of their narrative descriptions. They will start to describe the scenes as an internal perspective. You need to keep things external. Remember you are describing a scene in which an audience is outside looking in. Descriptions need to be kept to visual and auditory senses. Descriptions that delve into smell, taste, or touch cannot be used because the audience watching the film cannot feel those things.

Chapter 3:
Introduce Your Characters

Once your scene is set up you are ready to introduce the players of the story. Like building the visuals of the scene you need to build the visual of the characters before they speak a line of dialogue. The more descriptive and precise your character introductions are, the easier it is for your reader to become invested in getting to know them and following them along on their journey.

New Character in the script

Whenever you introduce a new character within the script you need to have certain elements in place to properly introduce them. First thing you need to capitalize their name, then follow it with an age description, a brief summary of their overall appearance, mood, or important features about them. Here is an example:

MARGARET, 75, a gray haired jolly woman who wears a frilly apron over her floral dress, pulls cookies out of the oven.

In this example I have described some of her appearance including her age, what she wears and an element of her physical appearance as well as her general mood. This paints a picture of her in very few words but enough for the reader to get a good idea of who she is. A good character introduction can immediately create an image of the character for the reader and allows them to see the scene unfold before them. More details of the character can be added in as you go but the introduction is the first impression that the reader receives.

Describing Emotions

One of the most difficult transitions from writing novels to writing screenplays is the way emotions are described. In a novel, the internal dialogue of a character can lay out exactly what the feel about a situation however screenplays are all visual and while a narrative voice over can accompany a character, that device has become over used and for many directors it looks like lazy writing.

So if you can't describe their internal thoughts how can you convey their reactions to the scenes? There are a couple of different methods but the key is to always convey it as a visual cue, not an internal cue.

Use Narrative Descriptions: The narrative descriptions are used for both the setting and the actions of the scene. If your character does something as an emotional reaction to the events in the scene, then use adverbs to explain how they react. Here is an example:

John walks into the living room and stubs his toe on the table. He howls in pain and angrily throws his plate of food on the floor.

By using emotional adverbs to describe their actions you are giving your reader a visual as to how the character appears on screen in that situation. One thing you don't want to do is describe their internal reaction. For example:

John walks into the living room and stubs his toe on the table. John is in immense pain and he becomes angry because of his stubbed toe. He howls at the injustice of the world and in a fit of rage he throws his plate of food on the floor.

While this second description is a bit over the top and funny, it also takes up more room on the page, where a simple description of his actions will do.

Use Parentheticals: Another way to describe the emotion of the character is to use a parenthetical under their character cue and above their line of dialogue. Parentheticals are emotional cues for the actors to use when they need to perform in that scene. Parentheticals can also be used to describe who the character is speaking to when there are multiple characters onscreen. A parenthetical is placed under the character name and above the dialogue and is spaced three spaces in from the dialogue. Here is an example:

JOHN

 (angry)

Ow! I hurt my toe!

When using parentheticals you must use them sparingly. Not every line of dialogue needs the parenthetical, only ones where the emotion of the line of dialogue may not be clear. If you have a scene where two characters are arguing it's easy to think that they are both yelling at one another, but if you want one of them to say something quietly or in a different emotion than expected then use a parenthetical for it. Parentheticals can also describe the characters movement as they talk but limit it to small movements or gestures. If a character makes several movements while they speak, then their dialogue needs to be broken up by longer action descriptions.

Extend Character Cues: When a characters dialogue is broken up by the action descriptions they will need another character cue and an extension on it to indicate that they are still talking. Here is an example:

JOHN

Ow! I hurt my toe.

John angrily throws his plate of food on the floor.

JOHN (CONT'D)

I hate stubbing my toe!

Chapter 4:
Dialogue 101

You have introduced your character and your setting and now comes what most professional screenwriters consider the hardest part of the script: dialogue. The reason it is so difficult? It is the tension between your characters and what connects the audience to your film. Good dialogue can make an audience laugh, make them cry, and make them connect with your characters on a deep level. Dialogue is the mark of a good screenplay and there are many pitfalls that both seasoned writers and newcomers fall into on a regular basis.

Pitfalls of Dialogue:

- **Overly Used Exposition:** This is when characters dialogue sounds like they are explaining the situation more than living within it. When dialogue is catered to explaining things to the audience, the scene becomes expository and forced. Exposition is needed in a script so the audience knows the context of the situation but it needs to come naturally within the dialogue of the characters.

–   **Exaggeration:** When writing your script your font and use of punctuation should be exaggerated to express emotion. Using all CAPITAL LETTERS to show someone yelling or using multiple exclamation points !!!!! should be avoided. If your character is shouting use a parenthetical but this should be done sparingly. Also the exaggerated use of explicit language can come across as lazy or unimaginative writing. Limit the F-bombs to characters or situations that are appropriate.

–   **Small Talk:** While we use small talk in our day to day lives (How's the weather? How are you? How are the kids?) this type of talk is very dull on screen because it lacks tension between the characters. Unless your scene has an underlying subtext try to avoid small talk and have your characters talk about deeper things.

–   **Repetition:** Having your character repeat something the audience already knows can drag down the script because it wastes valuable screen time. Unless it's a phrase that is used as a reference to a previous scene, make sure your characters aren't just repeating the same information over and over.

- On the Nose: When a character expresses exactly how they feel through the entire script, there leaves no room for tension or sub text. Characters need to be conflicted, there needs to be turmoil and their reactions need to have a deeper context. If your characters just say exactly what is on their minds then there is no suspense or drama to the scene

- Unoriginal Dialogue: It's easy to reference lines of dialogue from other films or media but you should avoid doing it in your own script. Having someone say "Hasta La Vista Baby" in your script pulls the audience out of story and it becomes very cliché. Avoid using common lines found in other films, it will make your dialogue stand on its own and unique.

- Talking Heads: When your characters speak their dialogue needs to be just as concise as your narrative descriptions. While it's fine to have a long speech sprinkled in, too much static dialogue on screen becomes dull and uninteresting. Make sure your characters are interacting physically, moving on screen and avoid lengthy conversations between characters.

It may work for Quentin Tarantino, but it might not work for you.

Chapter 5:
Common Mistakes and Faux Pas

As a professional script editor I have seen my fair share of bad writing and many new writers will make mistakes in their screenplays that are viewed in the industry as very unprofessional. When you are pitching your screenplay you want it to come across as professional and polished as possible. Here are some common mistakes and faux pas to avoid in your writing process.

Directing your Script:

Often times new writers will confuse a screenplay for a template for the director to use when making the film. They will add in camera shots, camera angles, editing techniques, or visual and sound effects. This is the biggest faux pas you can do in the industry and is a guarantee that your screenplay will never be produced. Why you ask? Because you are imposing your ideas on the director and cinematographer. Unless you are the director of the project and this script is the production draft, camera shots and effects need to be cut out of the screenplay. Instead you want to convey the story visually so that the director can visualize the shots as he reads it. Instead of telling the director to have a close up shot of a character, describe the anguish on the characters face. This will allow the director to map out the shots themselves and they are more likely to come on board the project.

Directing your Actors:

Once again this is a major faux pas because you are imposing on your actors and their abilities to emote within the scenes. The use of parentheticals should be sparse because you want the actors to be able to develop their own characters and how they respond in a situation. Often times when a actor seems to do poorly in a film it is because they have been restricted by the direction in the screenplay and couldn't develop their own take on the character.

Misuse of Punctuation:

This falls in the same boat as the exaggeration within the dialogue. The use of "..." as a beat (pause) in the dialogue can be done when there is a break in between the lines of dialogue. But using it throughout someone's lines comes across as a stutter or lazy writing. Incidentally, the use of "uh, ah, hmm" also gives off a bad impression. Once again trust your actors to make those small pauses and to stumble on their words.

Broken Sentences:

Nothing drives me more crazy as a script editor than a writer who uses incomplete sentences in their narrative descriptions because they think it will save them space on the page. Incomplete sentences in a script comes across as incredibly lazy writing and insulting to the reader. It doesn't take much to make it a complete sentence and if you are worried about saving space, then you need to rethink your writing entirely. Using incomplete sentences as a stylistic choice also comes across as pretentious and will turn off many producers and directors from your project

Wrong Scene Headings:

As I mentioned in the previous chapter scene headings are crucial to laying out your setting for each scene. Many new writers struggle with what constitutes a new scene and where they need to place their scene heading. The format of the scene heading never changes and they are not chapter titles which many novelists tend to think. Scene headings are used any time a character moves from one location to another and any time the setting or time of day is different. Scene headings are used by the production team to quickly sort out the scenes they have so they can produce them and any screenplay with improper scene headings will undoubtedly be passed on.

Chapter 6:
Perfecting Your Title and Revisions

Once your screenplay is complete the next stage is revisions and polishing it up so it looks professional and clean. Part of this is revising your first draft and the other is creating a clean polished title page.

Revisions:

Revising a screenplay can be a daunting process and sometimes it takes months or years until the screenplay is ready to produce. However if you started with a solid concept and a good outline and treatment then revisions can be a matter of fine tuning the details.

Fresh Eyes: After writing your first draft of your screenplay, you need to step away from it. Give yourself a few days and don't think about it. Better yet, give it to a friend or family member to read through it and give you their thoughts. The point is that when you write a script you become so involved with it that you can't really see that mistakes or plot holes. Coming back to it with fresh eyes helps clear you head and read it as if it is a fresh script.

Read it Out Loud: Reading your script out loud or in a group situation will help you catch the little mistakes that may be hidden within the script. Doing a table read with a group of actors will help you understand the flow of your dialogue and see the issues with pacing or your characters emotions.

Copy Edit: When it comes time to polish the script, you will need to find a copy editor. A copy editor proofreads the script and corrects all of the spelling, grammar and formatting issues your script may have. There is nothing worse then sending out a killer script that is rejected because of typos and spelling errors. Good copy editors will have a reasonable rate and it is worth the investment in order to have a perfectly polish script.

Title Page:

The last step to completing your script is to create the title page. If you have been in debate on the title of your film, then now is a good time to reflect upon the elements of the film to find a good title that will hook people in. Most movie titles keep it simple and sleek, one to five words in length and gives a good hint at what the film is.

When you settle on a title you will need to create a title page that will be placed on the front of the script. The title page needs to have the following:

- Title

- Written By:

- Revisions By: (if you had another writer do the revisions)

- Based On: (If your screenplay is based on source material)

- Contact information

- Copyright Date (if copyrighted)

The title of the script needs to be centered right in the middle of the page followed underneath by the authors name. Then the listing for revisions and based on are underneath that. The contact information however needs to be on the bottom left side of the page and needs to consist of the Contact name (Yours or your agents) the phone number and email address to contact and possibly a physical address. The Copyright needs to be at the bottom center of the page.

The title page should have no other information on it, no synopsis, no tagline, and no character lists. Your script should be able to stand on it's own enough, no additional notes are needed.

Once you have your title page and your polished screenplay you are ready to begin the process of getting it made.

Conclusion

Thank you again for purchasing this book!

I hope this book was able to guide you in proper industry standard screenplay writing.

The next step is to learn how to prepare your script and sell it so it can be produced. This is outlined in the next section of this series.

Finally, if you enjoyed this book, then I'd like to ask you for a favor, would you be kind enough to leave a review for this book on Amazon? It'd be greatly appreciated!

Thank you and good luck!

Book IV
30 Day Screenplay Challenge

Steps to Selling Your Script

By George Lucas

Introduction

I want to thank you and congratulate you for purchasing the book, *"30 Day Screenplay Challenge: Steps to Selling Your Script."*

This book contains proven steps and strategies on how to pitch your feature screenplay to movie executives, producers and more.

So you've completed your 30 day screenplay challenge. What's next? This book focuses on the next steps to turning your screenplay into a feature film. It outlines the steps you need to take in order to get your foot in the right doors and what do when you are offered a chance to sell your script. This book will help you with sending out your script to film festivals and competitions, creating a pitch package to sell your idea, meeting with agencies and business managers, how to overcome obstacles and road blocks, networking and promoting your script, and finally how to negotiate the sale of your script. The film industry is a complicated system and this book will help you get your script into the right hands in a fast and easy way.

Thanks again for purchasing this book, I hope you enjoy it!

Chapter 1:
Sending Out Your Script

You finally made it and completed your feature length screenplay. You've taken the time to revise it and polish it up and now you have that winning idea down on paper. But what comes next? Many people who write their screenplays end up putting them in a drawer and forgetting about them, never seeing their work truly come to life on screen. If every screenwriter did this, we would never have films to enjoy. Screenplays are written to be shared with others and used as a guide to creating an art form that can be enjoyed by millions. If you are passionate about the screenplay that you've created then you want to share it with the world. Getting your screenplay out can be rewarding and exciting but you want to make sure that you are careful.

There are several things you need to do before sharing your work with others.

Protect your work - The first step you want to take before sharing your story with the world is to protect it from plagiarism or outright theft. Sometimes people in the movie business want to cut corners and if they come across a new and inventive story they will steal the idea and sometimes even steal pages directly from the script. There are several ways to protect yourself from this happening.

Register Your Script - The first step is to register your screenplay with the Writers Guild. If you are in the United States you will register with the Writers Guild of America (WGA) with either the East coast or West Coast branch. Registering your script puts it in the WGA archives and gives you certificate that proves you are creator of your content that is time stamped on the day you register. This means that if another writer tries to steal your work, you have proof of registration prior to their claim and it will be valid in court and supported by the WGA. Registering your script with the WGA does not guarantee you membership with them, but it is a level of security that you want to put on your script before sharing it with others.

Copyright Your Script – Registering your script is the first step in protecting your work and doesn't really cover all of the legal bases. In order to be protected fully you want to copyright your work with the United States Copyright Offices. By copyrighting your screenplay, you are stating that this is your content and any one else claiming it is theirs can be legally sued for copyright infringement. Before sending your material out you want to have this in place as a good measure and both registration and copyrighting can now be done easily online.

Sending your work out

Once your screenplay is legally protected you want to cast out a wide net so that your script can been seen by as many people as possible. One way to do this is to enter it into screenplay competitions and film festivals to start generating a buzz about it.

Research Screenplay Competitions: It's easy to think about the major film festivals such as Sundance and Cannes, but there are thousands of competitions out there that are also successful and can help you gain some exposure. You'll want to research into film festivals and screenplay competitions that occur around the globe. This will help get your script out there and read by industry professionals. Some screenplay competitions offer script coverage which means for an additional fee they will read through your script and send back notes on your overall concept, characters, story line, and issues that they find within it. This is valuable feedback that can help your script stand out among the thousands of submissions that are sent in. In screenwriting you are never really done with revisions until the movie is released, so any notes that you get can be useful.

There are thousands of screenplay competitions and film festivals every year and now it has become easier than ever to search through them using websites such as Withoutabox.com. These search engine sites with go through all of the festivals and narrow down your search to find the ones that best meet your needs.

Build a Calendar of Submission Deadlines: Once you have found a good number of competitions and festivals that you want to submit to, build a calendar for all of the different submission deadlines. Festivals are year round and the deadlines for them are scattered all over. Create a calendar that lists the following:

Festival or Competition Name

Early Bird Deadline and price

Regular Deadline and price

Late Deadline and price

You'll find as the competition draws closer the price of submitting your work increases so it's good have the price listed for each of those dates so you can budget accordingly. Once your calendar is filled up you can look through it and plan ahead to submit to as many competitions as you can. Sometimes the prizes for the competitions are meetings with industry professionals or a chance to have the script made into a film. It's always worth it put your work out there in any way you can.

Chapter 2:
Create a pitch package

Once your screenplay has made the festival rounds and you have gathered some attention in the film industry you may be presented with the opportunity to meet with a movie producer or director who is interested in your script. Walking into those meetings you want to be ready to sell your idea and your story in way that will inspire them to move forward with the project. You need to be prepared in those meetings to be able to articulate your idea in an oral pitch. Even seasoned writers and directors still have to pitch their ideas to the movie studio executives and they have years of experience behind them. When you walk in you need to make a good first impression and have an articulated and well thought out idea. This is where a pitch package comes into play.

Start with the Synopsis: When you were first starting out your script, you created a tagline, logline, and synopsis. These are crucial in the pitch package and are the first thing that your potential investor reads. If your script has changed during the process you'll want to go back through and revise your tagline, logline, and synopsis to reflect the new changes. Your tagline needs to be bold, catchy, and intriguing and your logline needs to break down the story to the very heart of it. You want to intrigue them and then explain to them in simple words what the story is about. From there your synopsis or pitch treatment needs to be 1-3 pages and covers the overall story, introduces your characters, and sets up the plot. The synopsis should be laid out in a way that is quick and easy for them to read within a few minutes because if it's too long they won't bother to read it.

Oral Presentation: The producers or directors that you meet with generally don't have a lot of spare time so you need to prepare an oral presentation during this meeting. Generally, this is separate from your synopsis but you will say the tagline and logline and then go into the pitch. Your oral presentation needs to be about why this story should be made into a film. You need to address why you feel this is a marketable idea and how the characters and story can draw in the audience and inspire others. If your screenplay is a comedy you need to make them laugh, if its a drama, you need to inspire them, if it's horror, you need to give them goosebumps. Your oral presentation can explain some of the major plot points of the script but keep it simple and keep it under 5 minutes. After that, they may grow bored or interrupt you and you'll lose their attention.

Package Materials: Along with your synopsis and oral presentation you want to have supplemental materials such as character descriptions, setting descriptions, potential budget and investment, possible talent, and visuals.

1. **Character Descriptions**: Your character descriptions need to be about one paragraph each and give a little explanation into your characters back story and motivations. You don't want to detail their life story, but you want to explain how the character got to that point in their life when the film begins. You want to set up what their overall goal for the script is and how this will change their life.

2. **Setting descriptions:** Are generally half a page to one page in length and explain the setting in which the film takes place. If you are writing a historical bio-pic you'll want to give a brief overview on that time period and the major events that occurred. If this is a Sci-Fi or fantasy script then you'll want to explain the

realm in which your characters are living but keep it simple and easy to follow.

3. **Potential budgets and investment material:** Are generally done by a producer for an investor or studio. If you are pitching to a producer or director, then keep this material simple, just estimate how much you feel it would cost to produce this film. You need to be realistic with this number though so research into similar films and their budgets before throwing out a ballpark number. If you are pitching to an investor or studio, then you will need to get a producer or someone who is experienced with film budgets to help you develop a budget sheet and an investment strategy. The more organized you are in your initial budgeting the more likely they are to green-light the project.

4. **Potential talent:** Outlined in the pitch package can simply be actors and actresses that you feel would fit the roles. If you had a particular actor in mind when you wrote a character, then mention it to them so they can visualize this character as you speak. It doesn't guarantee that you will get that actor on board but it

gives them an idea of the caliber of stars they can cast in this film.

5. **Visuals:** Include photos or videos that you bring with you that will help you sell the idea. Drawings of concept art for the characters or setting help paint the picture for the potential investor. Pictures of talent or real life settings can help them see the potential in this idea and sometimes it's best to walk in with a trailer for the film so they can see the marketability of the film. Any trailer that you produce will not necessarily be the final trailer but it helps cement in the idea. I would stay away from bringing in costumes or props, unless you are prepared to explain why they are important to the pitch.

Chapter 3:
Get your foot in the right door

Most people think that the film industry has a very basic system in order to get ideas into production. You pitch to a movie executive and they either green-light the project or they don't. The reality is that reaching that point is a complicated network of agents, producers, directors, and business managers. There is a multitude of industry professionals whose jobs are to get you in the door and into that pitch meeting. So where do you begin?

Agents – If you have a script that has received some accolades through the film festival market you may already get the opportunity to work with an agent or business manager. However if that was not part of the prize package the next step to getting your foot in is to search for an agent for representation. The WGA website has a reference page of some of the top agencies in the United States but do some digging on your own. Research into professional writers and their representation who are similar to your writing style. This information can be found on their professional pages on IMDB.com or their personal website. Once you have a list of agencies that you are interested in, you need to send a query letter.

Query letter – These are one page letters to the agency that explain who you are and what your script is about. You want to keep this letter brief but also interesting so that they want to learn more about your idea. Usually you will provide the tagline and logline of your idea as well as reference any accolades that you have received. The letter is generally 1 to 2 paragraphs and at the end you tell them that if they are interested they can contact you for a copy of the script.

Business Managers – While agents may represent you for a specific screenplay, a business manager will help you build your writing career. They are similar to agents and sometimes overlap, but the business manager will help you find new projects to write for or help you secure a writing contract for a specific company. Business managers also require query letters and many times they will be referred to you by an agency. Agents deal with specific contracts between writers and production companies on specific projects. If you want someone to go up to bat for you repeatedly, hire a manager.

Chapter 4:
Stumbling over Road Blocks

Like every creative endeavor, there will always be obstacles and rejection and being a screenwriter means you have to have tough skin. When you create a script that you feel so passionately about it can be hard to hear criticism on it, and even harder when you are rejected by agents and studios. Even the most seasoned professionals still have projects that are not sold, or are put on the shelf and never get made. Sometimes you will deal with production studios that buy the rights to your work and then have others come in and change it so that your original work is not the same, and sometimes not as good. Unlike a novel where there is only two filters between the writer and the reader, Screenwriters deal with dozens of filters before their work is displayed on the silver screen. From the producers to the director, even down to the editor, a screenplay can be altered and changed so many times that sometimes it gets lost in translation. And that's even if you make it through the door. Here are some steps to take when you face rejection or challenges along the way.

Don't take it personal – It can be easy to get emotionally invested in your work and when someone comes along and says it's not up to snuff, it's easy to take it as a personal attack. If you are rejected by an agency, it's not because they feel your work is terrible, they may just not be interested in that type of story. Keep in mind that agencies hire people to read through the hundreds of query letters that are received every day, sometimes they are looking for something very specific. And sometimes things can just slip through the cracks.

Be tenacious – Don't give up after one rejection. Don't give up after 100. You need to keep trying and find different paths to getting your script sold. Robin Moore, the writer for the film *The French Connection* once said "I could wallpaper a room with the rejection letters." Sometimes it feels like that is all you will see, but if you keep going eventually you will find someone interested.

Continue to Write – Just because you have completed this first screenplay, doesn't mean you can't write another. In fact a lot of writers will tell you that their "big break" came from a script that they wrote for another project or was something that they didn't feel was as strong. A lot of times it's these smaller projects that will get your foot in the door and then your passion project comes later. So don't give up on writing, keep going. Maybe that silly script you wrote for practice or that script you wrote over a holiday will be the one that gets you noticed. When you do, you want to be ready to show them more work.

1. **Join a Writers Group:** Sometimes it can feel like you are the only one in the world who is struggling with this process and it can be really easy to feel down about it. There are so many others out there that are in the same boat as you, they have created something they feel passionate about but are struggling to get it seen. Joining a writers group can help you feel that you are not alone and the responses and feedback from your fellow peers can give you new insight into your situation. Check out your local library or community center to see if there is a group near you. Most of these groups are free to join and offer readings and critiques of your work. Their feedback can help you find the major issues with your script or help you find new and better ways to market it to agencies. Having a network of support of like minded individuals can help keep you going and

motivate you to push through your obstacles towards success.

Chapter 5:
Networking and Promotion

Sending out query letters takes time and often when you send them out cold, you never hear back from them. In the film business, the old saying "It's not what you do but who you know" is very on point. Many times it can be hard to break into the business just because you don't have the right contacts. Networking and promoting yourself as a writer can be just as important as writing your script.

Start local: Because of the rise in the independent market, every city and town will have some kind of local film industry within it. Check out local screenwriters groups, film festivals, or even local stage and theater companies. Chances are there are other writers in the same town and you can get to know them and learn from their experiences. If you live in a bigger city, there are generally Screenwriter Associations or independent Film Associations that host monthly meetings and workshops that are also good opportunities to get your name out there.

Business cards: I know this seems like such a small detail to cover but a business card will still get you far in the industry. If you are looking to sell a particular script or idea then you will want to incorporate that idea into the card. On the front of the card put your contact information under the title "Screenwriter" but then on the back put the title of your script and the tagline to try to reel them in. Make your card memorable and unique so that when you network at the local mixers you can hand them and people will remember your name and face and it may lead to new opportunities.

Build an Online Presence: You want to create a website page that you can direct people to that will give them more information on your screenplay and writing. The website page can be very simple but it needs to include some of the same material as your pitch package such as the tagline, logline, and synopsis. Then make sure to have a brief biography on you as a writer and your contact information. There are many website building platforms out there that are easy and free and this is a good way to intrigue potential producers or directors into contacting you for the script. Make sure to include your website name on your business cards so when you are meeting with new people you can hand them the card and they can go to the website to get more information.

Keep it Professional: The worst thing you can do for yourself as a writer is to gain a bad reputation. When you are out networking and socializing keep things professional and positive. You only have one first impression and you never know who will become a key to your success. While you may come across industry professionals who are not pleasant you don't want to burn any bridges. Be honest with the people you meet, you don't want to come across as fake or disingenuous but don't bash on other writers or industry professionals. Producers and directors are more likely to remember you if you make a genuine positive connection with them and you want to have a reputation in the industry as being professional and reliable.

Watch Out for Sharks: There are people in the industry who prey upon new writers to try to swindle them out of money or their creative content. You want to be wary of these "sharks" or con-men so to speak. Be wary of ANYONE who tells you that they will get your foot in the door if you give them money upfront. Real agents and business managers do not ask for money up front, they will take a commission from the sale of your screenplay so they are just as invested in getting it sold as you are. If you are approached by an agent or manager that says they take their commission up front, walk away. Chances are they are a scam and will take your money without hesitation. Because there are these types that float within the industry always make sure to research into the agent or company that approaches you. If they are a legitimate reputable agent then their information will be easy to find online so anyone who has no online presence or proof of their track record is just trying to make a quick buck off of you. As always keep it professional when you decline their offer, you can be cautious and courteous.

Chapter 6:
Negotiating the sale

So you have managed to pique the interest of a producer or director who wants to produce your screenplay. What comes next? Usually a producer or director is looking for a screenplay that they can pitch to a studio to get funding. These individuals or the studio they are working with will offer you an Option Agreement. This is a contract that allows that producer or director to obtain the rights to your script for a determined period of time so that they can produce it. There are three elements to an option script that you should be aware of:

The Option Period – This is time frame that you agree upon in which they have to get the project going. This is agreed upon by both parties but usually the director or producer will give you a ball park time frame. This time frame includes time for them to pitch it to a studio, gather together the team for the production and build the film's budget. Most Option Agreements have an extension that allows them extra time if they need.

The Option Payment – This is the price that you negotiate with the company for your payment up front. The option payment is a payment made to you to show they are serious about this project. At this point in time if you have agent representation, your agent would negotiate the price, but you if are not represented, then a good rule of thumb for your asking price is 10% of the purchase price (see below.) This part of the contract can be very tricky and a writer should never negotiate the price on their own. If you have someone who wants to option your screenplay then it's in your best interest to hire an agent or entertainment lawyer.

Purchase Price – This is the amount you will receive if the screenplay ever goes into production. Usually this amount is paid to you in full on the first day of principle photography. Generally this amount is determined based on the production budget for the film but sometimes you can get a set amount. For WGA writers their purchase price is generally negotiated at 10% of the total production budget. For non-WGA writers, it's anywhere from 2-5%. This is based on the writers experience and track record and so when you are starting out don't expect to receive WGA salaries but you want to make sure that you are not getting under paid. There are many companies out there that will try to swindle inexperienced writers into selling at a dismal rate which is why its so important to read the fine print. A good rule of thumb to consider is how much time you spent working on your screenplay from concept to final draft and total up the number of hours times an hourly salary that you feel is a good wage. Always remember to keep taxes and your agent's fees in mind when negotiating this price, as you can end up with a large chunk taken out for both.

Back End Points - Sometimes a writer can negotiate for something called "back end points." These are a small portion of the films profits when it distributed in theaters or on DVD or online streaming. Sometimes as a writer it may be good for you to take a smaller purchase payment up front in order to receive more back end points, especially if you think the film will do particularly well. The calculation of back end points is a very complicated process and you need to be aware of all of the different types of points there can be before accepting them as payment. Never cut your purchase payment out entirely, it is a huge risk and if the film fails you will be left with no income from your investment. As a screenwriter it is best to always get as much as you can up front since it is such a long process before the film reaches the screen.

You can see why it is so important to have legal and literary representation. When you are dealing with a studio that wants to buy your script, the purchasing price can sky rocket based on the budget and you need to know what you are entitled to before signing anything. Budgets that are in the millions can yield amount for the option agreement and professional screenwriters can make a very good living just from selling their scripts. Keep in mind that studios and producers are trying to make a profit so they will try to purchase your screenplay for the lowest price possible. It is perfectly normal to counter a producer's offer but you want to be reasonable with your asking price. Having an experienced agent on your team will get you the best the deal for you script and always do your homework. Find out what films that are comparable to yours were sold for and base your price on that.

Conclusion

Thank you again for purchasing this book!

I hope this book was able to help inspire you to continue on the journey to having your script made into a film. And who knows, maybe you will discover a passion for writing can build a career out of it. The road to getting your screenplay produced can be long and filled with obstacles. For some writers it takes years for them to catch their big break and many times people give up on their dream before it even reaches an agents desk. If you stay determined and keep going the reward of seeing your film on the silver screen is all worth it in the end. There is nothing like watching your film in a theater with an audience, it is both nerve racking and exhilarating. With these steps, you are on your way to achieving your dream and will one day get to feel the thrill of seeing your characters come to life.

If you have successfully sold your first feature script the next step will be for you to sell another and possibly one day join the Writers Guild. The guild offers screenwriters benefits such as insurance and a 401K so it's a great opportunity to make this your career.

Finally, if you enjoyed this book, then I'd like to ask you for a favor, would you be kind enough to leave a review for this book on Amazon? It'd be greatly appreciated!

Thank you and good luck!

Other Book by Author

The Step-By-Step Guide to Writing a Novel for Fiction writers and Novelist

or visit the URL below:

http://www.amazon.com/Step-Writing-Fiction-Writers-Novelist-ebook/dp/B00VR4NOKQ/ref=tmm_kin_swatch _0?_encoding=UTF8&qid=1444745957&sr=1-4

25556836R10074

Made in the USA
Middletown, DE
02 November 2015